START SOMETHING

You Can Make a Difference

**EARL WOODS
AND THE TIGER WOODS FOUNDATION
WITH SHARI LESSER WENK**

simon & schuster

new york london toronto sydney singapore

SIMON & SCHUSTER
Rockefeller Center
1230 Avenue of the Americas
New York, NY 10020

Simon & Schuster and colophon are registered trademarks
of Simon & Schuster, Inc.

Designed by Jeanette Olender
Manufactured in the United States of America

1   3   5   7   9   10   8   6   4   2

Library of Congress Cataloging-in-Publication Data is available

ISBN 0-7432-1096-4

ACKNOWLEDGMENTS

This book would not have been written without the persistent arrogance, humor, and love of my agent, Shari Lesser Wenk. Putting this project together was a work of joy and happiness: You're a good girl, Shari. Thanks, too, to Jeff Neuman and Simon & Schuster, who understood and supported the concept of this book and made it possible for children around the world to benefit from its content.

This book is dedicated to the millions of beautiful children all over the world who face life's trials and tribulations as they prepare to go forth into adulthood. Although their journey may be challenged by pitfalls and obstacles, my sincere wish is that it is also filled with understanding, sympathy, and lots of love. I hope that this book will assist them in their adventure.

Dear Friends,

I challenge you. I dare you.

I challenge you to be a winner. No, not in golf, but in your own life, in whatever you choose to do, whatever you care about. I challenge you to make a difference in the world, to reach higher and farther than you ever imagined. I challenge you to *start something.*

Are you up for it? Are you ready for the challenge of a lifetime? Because this challenge, if you succeed, offers rewards that will change the way you think, act, and live—forever. If you believe, like I do, that we all have the ability to make a difference in the world—in school, at home, with our families and friends, and within ourselves—then this book will get you started toward becoming a bigger, better person—a *role model.*

Let me introduce you to my role model, my hero: my dad. When I was a kid, he taught me to believe that anything is possible, and he's living proof that it's true. He has overcome so many obstacles in his own life, and he learned the hard way that big dreams can have beautiful results. By the time he was thirteen, his parents had died and he was left to be raised by his sister. Even though there was little money for him to go to college, he was determined to get his education, and because he was such a great athlete he earned a baseball scholarship to Kansas State University, becoming the first black baseball player in the Big Eight Conference. After his freshman year, he had the opportunity to become a professional baseball player, but decided instead to stick with school so he could get his degree. After graduation, he entered the Army and eventually joined the Green Berets (one of the most dangerous and demanding jobs anywhere), worked his way up to the rank of lieutenant colonel, and fought in the Vietnam War—twice. Later, while stationed in Thailand, he met my mom, and when they moved back to the

United States, they encountered racial prejudice, as he had his entire life. And then, of course, he ended up having a son who loves to play golf, a sport that had never really been open to minorities (and certainly not to three-year-olds!). I am overwhelmed by what he had to overcome to make it possible for me to achieve my goals. I say this with great pride: I wouldn't be where I am today without him.

Believe me: Whatever he's written in these pages, he's learned from experience.

In this book, you'll find many of the ideas and lessons he taught me when I was growing up. Now he and I want to pass them on to you, so that you can find ways to make them part of *your* life. I use these ideas every day, whenever I have to make a decision or solve a problem, whenever I'm feeling down or frustrated, whenever I'm not sure which way to turn. I have always discovered the right answer in the lessons you'll find in this book.

He also taught me the importance of reaching out

to others, helping people who are less fortunate, and sharing my success with them. The most important thing I've ever learned is to "share and care" for others, and you'll read about that a lot in this book. This concept inspired the Tiger Woods Foundation, the not-for-profit charitable organization that my dad and I created, with him as its president. Our goal is to reach out to kids just like you by supporting programs and organizations that can show you how to set goals for yourself and offer you the opportunity to turn your dreams into reality. We want to make a difference. Don't you?

As you'll see, my dad is a firm believer that dreams can come true, and I'm living proof that he's right. But he also showed me that nothing is possible if you don't work for it. That's what this book is all about: your commitment to create possibilities for yourself and for others. Nothing you read here will make you a great golfer. But if you're open to it, there is so much that will make you a great friend, a great teammate, a great son or daughter, a great brother or sister, a great student, and, most important, a great person. I hope that the suggestions and concepts you'll discover here will be as helpful and inspiring to you as they have been to me in my life.

I am committed to giving the best of myself. With your help, I believe we can make a difference in the lives of others across the world. I challenge you to join me. The time is now!

Your friend,

Tiger Woods

INTRODUCTION

Let me tell you a story. When Tiger was five years old, he and I were watching TV one night, and there was a news program about children starving in Ethiopia. It was horrible: babies who looked like skeletons, children dying from lack of food and water. Tiger just sat and stared at the terrible pictures.

"I have a friend from high school who became a doctor," I said, "and he's there in Ethiopia trying to help these kids." Tiger didn't say a word, didn't take his eyes away from the images on the screen.

When the program was over, he got up and disappeared into his room. He returned a few minutes later, carrying a small bag.

Inside the bag was his cherished collection of gold coins.

"Daddy," he said, "would you send these to your friend so he can help those kids?"

It was a moment I'll never forget. Tiger had learned one of the most important lessons you can learn in life: You have to share and care for others. He didn't have much to offer back then, but he knew that whatever he had, it was more than those starving children could ever dream of. He saw people in need, realized that he had the power to help, and wanted to make a difference.

This book is for you and about you, to help you discover your own power and use it to make a difference. You don't have to send gold to Ethiopia; you can make a difference everywhere you go, every day of your life. At home, at school, with your friends and family, on your team, within yourself, you have the power to reach out to others, to be a leader, to achieve incredible things, to be a role model. It all starts with you.

But how do you start?

When you were born, you were perfect. Everybody is. The problem is, no one has ever figured out how to stay that way. Life has a funny way of teaching us bad habits and letting us fall into ruts we can't get out of. We learn about fear, failure, disappointment, jealousy, insecurity, and selfishness. We absorb all this negative energy that keeps us from being strong and positive about who we are and what we can achieve. But if you're determined to overcome all that and become a role model in life—as Tiger has—then you will have unlimited opportunities to do whatever you set your mind to.

When people look up to Tiger and think of him as someone they admire, I hope with all my heart that it's not just because he's a great golfer but rather because he's a great person. No one deserves to be a role model just because he can hit a ball; you become a role model—a true leader—by working hard to succeed and showing others that they can succeed too, by being the kind of person that others want to be, by inspiring others to be their best and to try their hardest. That is Tiger's goal and it can be yours, too. You may not ever play golf like Tiger, but you can follow his example on your own road to success.

It's up to you to start something, *now!* In this book, you'll find dozens of ways you can start something new and change your world one step at a time. Some of it involves taking action; some just gives you a different way to see the things around you. Try a few or try them all. Just try!

Challenge yourself. Dare to stand out from the crowd, to set an example for others, to lead, to shine. You have powers that you haven't even discovered yet, deep inside you, waiting for you to release them. Let them out. Use them to make a difference in your life and in the lives of others. Use your power to care about others; to make solid, responsible choices; and to stand up for what you believe. Dare yourself to set goals that only you can achieve. You are a miracle and you can make miracles happen. Celebrate yourself, love yourself, for all the things that make you special and unique. You are beautiful and wonderful, and I love you.

—Earl Woods
Cypress, California, 2000

START SOMETHING

Something Good Happened to You Today—Did You Notice?

It's so easy to get caught up in daily problems: Your parents are mad at you, your best friend made plans that didn't include you, that math test was impossible, you didn't make the team. Yet believe it or not, in the middle of all that stress and trouble, there are wonderful things happening all around you, if you take the time to notice. Every day, take a minute to think of three *good* things that happened. They can be big events, like winning a game or getting a good grade. Or they can be small, hard-to-notice things, like hearing a good joke, receiving a compliment, or making a new friend. Even on your worst days, you can still appreciate your favorite stuffed animal, a long bike ride, or your good health. Don't let yourself get lost in your problems—focusing on a few positives will keep your head above water even in the toughest times.

What Do You Believe?

As you probably know, Tiger was born half African American and half Asian, and he is proud of both aspects of his heritage. Yet he is constantly pressed by both groups to "choose" which he is, as if there's a prize for the winning team. Through it all, Tiger has held on tightly to his conviction that he is "both," and nothing can shake that loose. It is one of his "core values," and we all need them to help guide us through life.

Core values are at the heart of every decision you make, every opinion you develop. They're an expression of what you believe, and they provide the foundation for your reaction to everything that happens in your lifetime.

What do you believe? Maybe you believe that you're smart, your parents love you, you're a good person, and you're generous. You might believe that there are angels in heaven, poor people should be helped, lying is stupid, and your red hair is cool. Identify your beliefs and let them guide you through your life. Be strong and determined to never lose sight of them. Remember, they belong to you and you alone: No one can ever take them away from you.

TIGER SAYS . . .

"I am the product of two great cultures. On my father's side I am African American. On my mother's side, I am Thai. My parents taught me to always be proud of my ethnic background. That will always be the case, past, present, and future. I feel very fortunate, and equally proud to be both African American and Asian."

Follow Your Passion, Not the Pack

Everyone is trying out for the school play—but you'd rather be in the band. Maybe all your friends are playing soccer, but you want to play tennis. Should you follow the pack, or follow your passion? It's hard to break away from your friends, especially if "everyone" is doing something together. But if you're lucky enough to know what you like, don't you owe it to yourself to stick with it? Your friends' interests don't have to be the same as yours. Why spend time on something that doesn't interest you, when you can devote yourself to something you really care about? When Tiger was a kid, no one else his age was golfing—but golf was his passion, and he wasn't afraid to stand apart from his friends to pursue it.

It takes a strong person to break away from the rest of the group, but you'll be glad you did. You can go to their soccer games, and they can watch you play tennis. What's wrong with that?

TIGER SAYS . . .

"Golf is definitely cool now, but it wasn't when I was a kid. But I kept doing it, because I loved it. I played other sports, but I didn't have the same passion."

Help a Little Kid

Remember how it felt to be little? There were so many things you didn't understand or couldn't do, and all those big kids thinking they're so great. Well, now that you're older and more experienced, it's your chance to be a real hero. Use your new maturity to help those younger than you. Instead of making a little kid feel stupid and helpless, make a point to say hi, share your seat on the bus, hold a door open, help him find his way around school, show her how to do something better. Give a kid a reason to look up to you. Wouldn't you appreciate the same kindness from those who are older than you?

TIGER SAYS . . .

"People took the time to help me as a kid, and it made a real impact on my life. I want to do the same for other kids."

Are You Ready to Make Your Own Decisions?

Now that you're growing up, you want to make some decisions for yourself and have more control over your life—what you wear, who you hang out with, how you study, what you do for fun. And that can be tough on parents, especially when they still want to be involved in those decisions. But there are steps you can take to earn your independence, and still keep your folks involved in your life. First, be thankful that your parents care enough to be concerned—that's their job. Second, discuss your choices with your parents. Let them know why you feel the way you do, honestly and maturely, without being defensive or angry, so they know that you've given careful thought to the decisions you're making. If they disagree, respect them enough to listen to their viewpoint. You may not agree with them, but if you want them to respect your opinions, you have to respect theirs. Finally, let your parents know that you'd like to try it your way and see how it goes—and that if it doesn't work out, you'll be honest enough to admit you need to go in a different direction. Your parents will respect your openness, and you'll show that you've earned the right to make choices for yourself.

Make a List of Things You're Good at

You might be the best artist, or athlete, or student in your class, but you won't be for long if you don't keep finding ways to improve. How good a golfer would Tiger be if he didn't learn new things or develop his skills? Sure, he'd have his basic talent, but he'd never know how good he could be if he didn't strive to learn, to grow, to improve.

You have room to grow, too. Write down all the things you're good at: Maybe you're a fast reader, or a talented artist, or a good baseball player, or a funny joke teller. First, congratulate yourself on your talents—they belong to you and no one can ever take them away. Then look at your list: Challenge yourself to get to the next level. Can you read one extra book? Draw a new animal? Catch more fly balls? Learn three new jokes?

Create new goals for yourself. Dare yourself to take the next step. How good can you be? That's up to you, isn't it?

TIGER SAYS . . .

"I just keep trying to improve as a player, which is something I have been able to do my whole life. That doesn't mean that I'm going to get better, but I have to keep trying. If I can look back on my career and say I improved every year, I'll be a happy man."

Read for Twenty Minutes Every Day

I know how busy you are: If you had a spare twenty minutes, you'd probably rather watch TV or listen to your new CD. But if you don't set aside regular time to read, you're cheating yourself out of amazing opportunities. All of the knowledge of the world is written. Anything you're interested in—sports, animals, art, poetry, history, space, movie stars, presidents, volcanoes, dinosaurs, music, stories—they're all there for you. Read a book, a newspaper, a magazine. Read fiction or nonfiction, paperback or hardcover. It will make you smarter, and take you to places you've never been and introduce you to people you've never met. We're so fortunate to live in an age of massive amounts of information, with unlimited access to all the world's knowledge and creativity. Use it and grow.

Did You Help Someone Today?

Wherever you live, wherever you go, there are people who need your help: the elderly man or lady who can't rake the leaves or wash the car, that kid who just fell off his bike and looks hurt, the mother who needs someone to watch her kids so she can run to the grocery store. Isn't there something you can do? Not for money, but just because you're a good person with a big heart? You can make an unforgettable difference in someone else's life, by giving just a little of your time and energy. And the person you helped will never forget it.

It's so easy to get lost in our own little worlds, worrying about our own problems. You can do better than that. Take a minute to look around you and notice other people. You have the power to reach out, to care. Use it to help others, and let others help you when you need it. That's what we're here for.

The Truth Hurts—but Lying Can Hurt You Even More

Anyone who has ever told a lie usually learns two things: (1) It's hard to keep the story straight, and

(2) liars usually get caught. It can be so tempting to lie, especially when the truth isn't very pleasant and the punishment is even worse. But what a waste of energy—not only do you have to worry about the thing you're lying about, but you have to remember the lie as well.

It takes a brave, strong person to stand up and admit the truth, particularly when the truth is going to land you in deep trouble. But the surest way to lose the respect of your friends and family is to be a liar. It takes a very long time to regain that kind of respect.

Everything in our universe is based upon truth. Don't be the exception.

Unload Your Past Mistakes

Get over it already! Do you think Tiger would ever win a tournament if he let his mistakes wipe out his focus and concentration? He learned a long time ago that mistakes can only mess you up if you let them. Don't let it happen to you. If you're still stuck on the last time you struck out, or the spelling test you didn't do so well on, you have two choices: Continue to beat yourself up for making mistakes (in which case you're destined to repeat them), or admit you made mistakes, learn from the experience, and grow.

Take a hard look at your performance: Did you give your best effort? Did you study hard enough for the test? Did you practice before the game? If yes, then maybe you just had an off day, and you have a great chance of succeeding next time. If the answer is no, then you know what you have to do to improve. Accept that you aren't perfect, learn from the experience, and move on. Try not to make the same mistake twice, but since you're human you probably will, and that's okay, too. Feeling bad about past experiences won't make new ones any better. Give yourself a fresh start—you deserve it.

TIGER SAYS . . .

"Too many people get caught up in the last bad shot they hit. I say it's more important to let go of what just happened and let each shot be a new one."

Shut Down the Jerk Who Teases You

If you've ever been picked on or teased, you know what a helpless, lousy feeling it is when a bully decides you're the target. When Tiger was a kid, he was picked on a lot. Not only was he a minority, but he was biracial, in a predominantly white school. And he played golf, which very few kids did back then. So he became an easy target for jerks who didn't like anyone who was different from themselves. That's what teasers are. Teasers manage to find something you can't change—your hair, your height, your

name—and make it your worst problem. But understand why people tease: They're cowards. Teasers are
so weak and insecure that they have to hurt someone
else just to feel better about themselves. The only
way they can feel powerful is to make someone else
feel small. And they usually make the whole mess
worse by throwing in, "Can't you take a joke?" as if
it's your fault that you got hurt by their cruelty.

So if you're the victim, how do you put an end to
it? Stop taking it. Tiger discovered—and you will
too—that the teaser picked *him* because he thought
he'd get away with it—he didn't think Tiger would
stand up and shut him down. But Tiger was better
than that, and so are you. Don't you believe in yourself enough that you don't really care if someone
makes fun of your curly hair or your long name? Instead of showing that he got to you—because that's
what he's waiting for—shut him down. Look at him
like he's nuts, shrug, walk away. Make *him* feel like
the fool, because, remember, that's his fear. If he

keeps going, tell him this: "You have your opinion, but I don't have to listen to it. I feel sorry for you that you have nothing better to do. But I do. See ya." And walk away. Make him feel like the fool he is. You have unlimited power—use it. No one can make you feel small without your permission.

It's Okay to Cry

Let's just admit it—we all cry. Yes, even you, and even your best friend who tries to look so tough.

Tiger cries, too. So what? For some reason, it's perfectly acceptable in our crazy society for girls to cry, but when boys cry, they never hear the end of it. So this one is for the guys, because girls seem to know this from an early age.

Somehow, we got the ridiculous idea that boys who cry are weak. That's as silly as saying that people who laugh are weak. After all, laughing and crying are just human reactions to life situations, and when they need to pour out, they just do. That's how emotions work. Hurt feelings, losing a game, sad movies, disappointment . . . they can all lead to tears. So can happy things, like a great victory or graduation day. But boys get the message that it just isn't macho or cool for boys to cry. And that's a shame, because people who cry aren't showing weakness, they're showing strength, courage, and honesty. Letting those emotions out proves that you're confident enough to be honest about how you feel, that you have the power to release your feelings instead of keeping them locked inside like a nasty secret.

You can be sure that no one laughed at Tiger when he cried after winning his first Masters, and he sure wasn't embarrassed. Crying makes you flexible, lets you bend without breaking. It releases tension and gives you a fresh perspective on what's really important to you. Learn to let it go. You'll never regret it.

TIGER SAYS . . .
"The best advice I ever got was from my dad, and it wasn't about golf: Always be yourself."

Compliment Someone

"I like your shirt." "Nice shot." "You're really good at that." It takes so little and means so much. Doesn't it make you feel good when someone compliments you? Well, spread it around. Not only does it make

others happy, it shows that you're confident enough to try to make others feel good about themselves. Compliments show that you appreciate someone else's effort and ability. It takes nothing away from you. A true compliment is honest and sincere—if you try too hard you'll sound phony. Just a few words from the heart do the trick.

Instead of Buying Gifts, Create Your Own Gifts of Good Deeds and Promises

Anyone with a few dollars can buy a gift, but it takes real creativity and generosity to give a gift from the heart. Wouldn't your parents love a book of coupons offering your services for a few extra chores? How about a certificate that lets your friend decide which movie to see or where to eat? For your sister's birthday, promise to make her bed, or let her borrow that

CD she loves. Or write a letter from the heart, telling someone special how important he or she is to you. There are a million things you can do that don't have monetary value but are sentimental and express how you feel about a person. Use your imagination. Let your love come out and truly share yourself. The lucky recipient will treasure it forever.

TIGER SAYS . . .

"The best present I ever got was the time my dad and I played golf Christmas Day, just the two of us, and that was pretty cool. I will always cherish that memory."

Whatever Problems You Have, Someone Else Had Them First

You are a unique and special person—there is no one else exactly like you in the entire world. The same is not true of your problems; no matter how badly you feel things are going for you, no matter how confusing and complicated your life seems, you are not the first person to experience what you're going through. All kinds of people are dealing with the very same issues right this minute. Now, this doesn't take anything away from your own troubles—if you think you have a problem then you definitely do—but it might make you feel better to know that other people have been there and understand how you feel. Talk to others about what's bothering you; share your concerns with people who have ideas and knowledge you can use. Let yourself learn from the experiences of others. Let them help. You are not alone in this world.

You Can Pick Your Friends, but You Can't Pick Your Brothers and Sisters

Okay, they take your stuff without asking, hog the phone and the remote control, pester you when you have friends over, and generally get in your way. The older ones boss you around; the younger ones follow you around. And who knows what they think about you! But they're yours—forever. Get to know them, because believe it or not, you will probably know them longer than any other people you will ever know. Think about it: They've been there since you were a baby, or you've been there since they were, and they'll still be there throughout your entire life. So even if you wouldn't choose them right now as best friends, think about how much you share with them: your family memories, relatives, experiences, and stories, both good and bad. They're part of your life history, and that can never be taken away from you. So make the best of it. Learn to get along and cooperate. Respect them and give them a reason to respect you. Be there for them when they need you. And if you're fortunate, you'll have built-in lifelong friends you can always count on.

You Are a Leader

Leadership is within each and every one of us. It doesn't mean you have to be a loud, shouting "Follow me!" type; you can do it with quiet dignity. You never hear Tiger telling people what to do or how to live their lives, but he shows it every day in the way he conducts himself, with class and dignity, and respect for others. There are many ways to lead—by your words, your actions, your attitude. The choice is yours. No matter what, when you're a good person, you *automatically* become a leader, setting an example for others to follow. You're strong, you're confident, you're poised. Gone are the days when you blindly followed someone else. You have the ability to question. You have the intelligence to challenge the answers. The one thing you must always remember: Leadership is a responsibility. And you can handle it.

TIGER SAYS . . .

"Being a role model means more than having others look up to you. A role model is someone who accepts responsibility for getting others to do great things."

Protect Your Planet

We all know how precious our world is: Every time we go outside, every drop of water we drink, every breath we take, we're relying on our environment to keep us safe and healthy. But we can't count on others to keep it that way—we all need to share the responsibility, and it starts with you.

Commit to three things you can do *every day* to help the environment and conserve energy. You can turn out the lights when you leave a room, shut off the television when you're not watching, pick up a piece of trash (even if you didn't drop it); turn off the water while you're brushing your teeth, don't pick flowers that aren't yours to pick. Do your part—make sure others do their part as well. We all want to live in a wonderful environment, on this great planet that we all share. Let's just do it.

You Have to Start Somewhere

Big hopes and dreams can feel overwhelming if you only focus on the end result. When Tiger won the U.S. and British Opens in the summer of 2000, his goal was, naturally, to win—and win big. But he couldn't focus only on breaking records and holding a trophy—he had to play four rounds of golf, 72 holes, one at a time.

Everything starts with a first step. That 400-page book you have to read for class? You read the first page, and then each page after that, one at a time. The championship trophy you want to win? You play your first game, and then play each game after that, one at a time. Reaching your goals is like climbing a ladder: You can't get to the top in one step. But if you plan your course and take charge of your plan, you'll be taking your first big step up the ladder. And when you feel like you'll never get to the next step, don't give up—just take a smaller step. You *will* get to the top, if you want it enough. It's up to you.

TIGER SAYS . . .
"I know what I want to accomplish, and I know how to get there. The ultimate goal is to be the best."

Hitting a Ball Doesn't Make
Someone a Hero

Tiger has often been called a "role model," which is an honor and responsibility he takes quite seriously. But is that because he's an awesome golfer, or an awesome person? I hope it's not because he can hit a ball and win tournaments and look great on TV. Just because someone is famous doesn't automatically mean you should look up to him. He might be a great golfer (or football player, or singer, or whatever), but it's what someone does away from the game—in real life—that qualifies him or her for role model status. After all, what is a role model? Someone who sets an example you can learn from and follow, someone who behaves in a way that makes you think about how you want to behave, someone who has the qualities we respect and admire. Can you learn all that by watching someone hit a ball?

Tiger is proud to be called a role model, not because he wins golf tournaments, but because he works hard to give back to the community, to uphold what he believes in, and to help others be the best they can be. Before you decide to follow someone else's example, make him or her earn it. Who in your life do you respect so much that you want to learn from them? If all you want to learn about is dunking a basketball, then go ahead and find an athlete to admire. But if you're looking for a role model who can show you how to get through life and be a good, successful person, look at those around you who have already made it: your parents, family members, teachers, coaches, friends, famous people (yes, including athletes) who do things you respect and admire, anyone who has had a positive impact on *your* life. Let those people have the honor of being your role models. Then go ahead and admire superstar athletes for what they are: superstar athletes.

TIGER SAYS . . .

"I don't consider other athletes to be my role models, although I admire them for their abilities. My own role model is my dad."

Notice the Kid Everyone Ignores

Life is easy—when you're the most popular, athletic, good-looking, successful kid at school. But what about the rest of us? What about the kid who always seems to be left on the outside, just watching? You know who I mean: You see him but you look right through him. You're not unfriendly, but you're not exactly friendly either, right? Believe me, it's a lonely, sad existence. Just imagine going through a day without anyone to talk to, no one to sit with, nobody interested in what you say or do. Please, reach out to these people. It may not be your responsibility to make sure every kid in school is included in every activity, but a simple friendly gesture from you can really make a difference. Include them in your conversations, say hello, make a little room for them in your group. Respect them as people. Respect them so they can respect you. Show you have the confidence to reach out and care about someone. You never know: You may make a great new friend.

TIGER SAYS . . .

"One of my goals and passions is to help people and I love doing it."

Don't Spread Rumors

Would you like somebody talking about you behind your back, spreading lies, half truths, and rumors? If the answer is no, then why do it to someone else? Not only is it mean and hurtful, it truly takes away from who you are as a person. People who spread rumors are just showing their own insecurities—they have to make someone else look bad so they can feel better about themselves. Aren't you better than that?

You have the power to stop yourself and others from gossiping. First, and most obvious, make the commitment to stop repeating stories you've heard about others, whether you think they're true or not. Is it your business? Does it have anything to do with you? If not, you're just being rude and mean. Imagine the girl you're talking about walking up behind you while you're entertaining your friends with a story you just heard about her. How would you feel? Embarrassed, at least, and probably a lot worse.

Show that you have the self-control and dignity to stop talking about things that don't involve you. You can stop listening, too, to blabbermouths who gossip and spread rumors. You can walk away; you can say, "That's not nice"; you can challenge the gossiper to admit that he or she doesn't really know whether the story is true or just a big fat lie. You can be the one to set a good example by using your power to do the right thing.

Adopt a Needy School

Somewhere in your community, or nearby, is a school where the kids don't have what you have. Maybe they could use some new books for their library, school supplies for the classrooms, or sports equipment for the playground. There are kids who need hats and gloves in the winter. What a difference you can make by organizing a collection for them in your class, your school, your neighborhood. It can be as big as you dream it to be. Your teacher or principal can help you spread the information to your school and community, so others can dream along with you. All you need are a few big cardboard boxes for people to drop their donations into, some willing volunteers, and a big heart. And here's the best part: Not only will you make a permanent impact on the lives of these special kids, you'll also be showing those around you how easy it is to share and care about others. What a great way to start others thinking about how they can make a difference, too!

TIGER SAYS . . .
"I want every child in America to have the opportunity I had."

No One Wins Every Time

It's the privilege of winners to announce, "We're number 1!" after a victory. Unfortunately, we never hear the other guys yelling, "We're number 2!" Too bad, because finishing second can be pretty impressive, especially in a sport like golf, where dozens are competing, and this week's number 1 will be number 3 or number 7 next week.

Do you realize how small that little spot is up there? There can only be one number 1. Everybody else has a bigger number. One person gets to win and a whole bunch don't. So what if you're second? Don't you think it's impressive that only one other person or team was better than you? Of course, we all want to win, and we set our sights on first place, championships, and gold medals. But if you've given everything you've got, held nothing back, and tried your best, then there is nothing wrong with not being number 1. Focus on your effort and performance, rather than on holding a trophy. Play hard, give your all, and the rest will take care of itself. Losing with dignity and maturity makes you a winner every time.

"I'm trying to get better. I'm trying to work on every facet of my game. I'm trying to improve to give myself chances in each and every tournament I play in."

Respect Your Body

You have one life, and one body. It seems obvious that you should do anything possible to avoid damaging either. Unfortunately, the world presents you with many opportunities to bring harm to both.

By now you know that the worst things you can put into your body are drugs, alcohol, and cigarettes. And believe me, once you get started, it can be nearly impossible to stop. The question is: Do you respect yourself and your body enough to say no to these poisons? Drugs, alcohol, and cigarettes are an insult and a joke to anyone who cares about being healthy, intelligent, and successful. They have never made anyone smarter or healthier and most definitely have damaged the lives and bodies of so many.

Like many kids, you'll probably find yourself in tough situations where you'll be pressured to "try it" or "have some fun." You are not alone. There are so many other kids who feel the way you do, that drugs, drinking, and smoking aren't for them. If you're honest and open and aren't afraid to talk about it with your friends, you'll see how many have the same doubts and concerns as you. Be strong enough to set an example they can follow, so they can make the same choice as you. Trust your parents enough to discuss the situation with them as well. Believe it or not, they may have faced the same issues.

You are working so hard to be positive, to do good things in the world . . . doesn't your body deserve the same commitment? It is where you live. You are the only one who can take care of it. It is you. Respect it and be proud of it. And above all, refuse to abuse it.

Get Along with a Tough Teacher

We all remember our favorite teacher, but tough teachers are just as hard to forget. Seems like they're always picking on you, never happy with your work, grading you harder than anyone else in the class. Maybe you're right (all teachers are not created equal); maybe you're being overly sensitive (would your teacher seem so mean if you were getting straight As?). Either way, you're stuck.

Now you have two choices: You can go to class every day with a bad attitude and blame your teacher if you do poorly, or you can try to find a way to make it work. The choice you make will mean the difference between a terrible learning experience, or a shot at a good one.

Keep in mind that your teacher is there for one reason: to teach. Not to be your best friend (although that's a nice bonus) or to solve your personal problems (also a bonus). You, on the other hand, are there to learn. It's as simple as that. Your responsibility is to get along with the teachers. You don't have to like them, but you do have to learn what they're trying to teach you. Try approaching your teacher privately, to discuss your concerns about your grades, or ask what you can do to improve. Most important, though, respect the job your teacher has to do, and be sure you do yours. Teachers are there to teach . . . you are there to learn.

Put Your Allowance to Good Use

If you're responsible enough to earn money, you're responsible enough to make some smart decisions about what to do with it. Do you run out and blow every penny as soon as you get it? Are you saving it all for something big? Are you setting some aside to give to a worthy cause? Here's a plan that can really work for you. First, put all of your money into one pot: allowance, money earned from baby-sitting or chores, birthday gifts, everything. Then divide the pot into three parts—money to save, money to spend, money to donate to charity. You can split it into equal parts, or give more to charity or savings. You can even decide to put aside some of your spending money for charity or savings. Any way you slice it, you're making the most of your money: helping yourself, and helping others.

Are You Too Critical?

The next time you find yourself about to criticize something or someone, ask yourself, "Am I doing this to be helpful? Or am I being mean? Will my comment be appreciated, or hurt someone?" Your answer means the difference between being a good friend and being plain rude. Are you commenting on some-

thing that can be changed or controlled (like too much perfume or talking during a movie), or are you pointing out a shortcoming that can't be improved (like big feet or a weight problem)? If you're truly trying to help someone, and you really do care about his or her feelings, think about how you'd feel if you were told the same thing. Be kind and sensitive, and let your friends know you're not picking on them or trying to hurt their feelings. And if you can't find a way to get your point across gently, maybe you should keep it to yourself.

Take Responsibility for Yourself

If you make a mess, clean it up. If you borrow something, return it. If you make a promise, keep it. If you start something, finish it. If you hurt someone, apologize. The only person who can take responsibility for your actions is you. No one else can make you be on time, turn in your homework, be friendly, or play fair—it's up to you, and you alone. Whenever you find yourself about to make an excuse or blame someone else for a problem, ask yourself, "Did I really do the right thing? Is there something I should be fixing?" If the answer is yes, step up and fix it. It takes a big person to accept responsibility without being told what to do. You're ready, and you can do it.

TIGER SAYS . . .
"Golf is not everything. It never will be. The most important thing is furthering yourself, making yourself a better person."

It's Okay to Be Nervous

Being nervous is a part of being a kid—nervous about a test, the big game, the school dance. But ask real winners about being nervous, and they'll tell you that the crazy feeling in your stomach shows that you really care, that you're really trying. It tells you you're about to do something great. Tiger still gets nervous before every tournament, just like he did when he was a kid. I never tried to talk him out of it. He understood, and you should too, that it's just a natural emotion, not a weakness. And if you really believe in your heart that you're a winner, you can turn those nerves into something great.

TIGER SAYS . . .
"People often ask whether I get nervous. Of course I do! If you don't, you shouldn't be out here. I almost always get nervous on the first tee and it usually lasts for a few holes. But I always have inner peace on the golf course. I try to stay calm and never let anything get to me."

Complaining Is for Cowards

When you're a complainer, nothing is ever good enough. It's too hot, the food stinks, the lines are too long, the test was unfair. Do yourself a favor: If you ever find yourself slipping into this pattern, do anything and everything to stop yourself, *immediately*. Not only does it make you sound so negative, depressing, and immature, but that attitude brings down everyone else around you as well. It's bad enough to complain about problems that have no solution—the weather, for example—but it's even worse when someone complains about a problem that, with a little effort and positive thinking, could be fixed instead of whined about. A true leader looks for the positive in any situation, cuts through the crabby grumbling, makes the best of tough situations, and gets results. Best of all, a true leader shows others how to do the same. You can do it, too.

Don't Wait for Holidays to Show You Care

We have Mother's Day, Father's Day, birthdays, and a calendar full of holidays that remind us it's time to give gifts and "show that you care." Why wait for holidays? Life is about caring every day. What good is a card one day a year when you show nothing the other 364 days? Presents and flowers and cards are nice symbols of our feelings, but only if we back them up with real caring in our day-to-day lives.

A few years ago, I was honored to receive the National Father's Day/Mother's Day Council's Father of the Year Award on Father's Day, and someone asked, "How do you and Tiger celebrate Father's Day?" My answer: "We don't, because we celebrate Father's Day *every* day." Of course, we celebrated extra hard last June when Tiger was kind enough to win the U.S. Open on Father's Day. As he said, "Not a bad gift." And one that I was certainly proud to accept.

But Tiger and I honor each other every day, no matter where we are, even when we haven't spoken in a couple of weeks. Try this in your own life. Honor the people you love every day. Show your "holiday spirit" all year, instead of waiting for the right day or season to come along.

Are You Listening?

There is hearing, and there is listening. It takes no effort to hear someone speaking, but it takes a real commitment to actually *listen* to what they're saying—and the other person can always tell which you're doing. Hearing means it went in one ear and out the other, without stopping at the brain for processing. Listening means it got your attention: not only did you hear it, but you processed the information and retained it. True listening says that you care, you're involved, the other person matters to you, you're willing to help, and willing to learn. What better way to be a great friend and great person?

The "I Can Do Better" Checklist

Nobody's perfect . . . not even you. Everyone can find ways to improve, if you're ready to be honest with yourself. Sit down and make a list of three things you'd like to work on, things you'd like to be better at. Maybe you'd like to keep your locker neater, or remember to turn in your homework on time. Maybe you'd like to raise your hand more often in class, or improve your jump shot. Look at each item on the list and plan how you can approach each one. It's hard to admit the things we're not good at, but you can't improve if you can't face the truth. Instead, feel proud that you're willing to make the effort. Be positive, don't beat yourself up, and above all, be honest. Keep checking the list, and when you've mastered each one, add new things to conquer. Be sure to offer yourself a reward for each goal you reach—you'll be amazed by what you can do if you make a plan.

TIGER SAYS . . .

"You're going to make mistakes. The key is to learn from them as fast as possible, and make changes as soon as you can. That's not always easy to do because ego and pride get in the way, but you have to put all that aside and look at the big picture."

Be Kind to Animals

Treat all animals as you would like to be treated. After all, you are an animal, too.

Say Hello

It's so simple: just say it. That tiny little word—"hi"—packs so much power. Why not use it? You probably pass ten people every day who you know, but never acknowledge. What's stopping you? Maybe you're afraid of sounding dumb, maybe you're embarrassed. But realize that all of us, you included, love to be recognized, and it doesn't get any simpler than a quick "hello." It only takes a moment, but its impact lasts all day. Reaching out to others says so much about who you are—it says that you're confident, you're nice, you're happy. It makes others feel good about themselves, and good about you, too. Make a commitment to just say "hi." And don't forget to answer if someone says it to you first.

If You Don't Know the Answer, Ask for Help

One of the biggest problems we humans have is admitting we don't know something. How many times have you nodded along with others, trying to look like you really understand, when all along you don't have a clue? Well, here's a newsflash: No one on this planet has all the answers. Not your parents, not your teachers, not your best friend, not you. It isn't a reflection on your intelligence to ask someone to explain something to you. Especially in school: I guarantee you, at least half the other kids don't know the answer either.

The beautiful thing about Tiger, when he was a kid, was that he always had enough confidence to ask, "What does that mean?" He never worried that he might sound stupid or weak. Instead, he showed that he was willing to learn, that he was strong enough to admit he didn't know something. As a result, he was never embarrassed to ask questions. The smartest people are those who are always asking questions. You can be one of them.

TIGER SAYS . . .

"My goal and objective is to learn something from every round of golf I play, whether it's a weekend round of golf at home or a practice round or a tournament."

Write Grandma a Letter

Don't you love to get mail? Of course, now that so many people use e-mail, most of your written communication probably comes through your computer. Well, what about folks who don't use computers, like your grandparents or other special people? They're probably not hearing "You've got mail!" five times a day.

So make their day: Sit down and spend five minutes writing a real letter. It doesn't have to be long, it just has to show you care. A few sentences about what's up with you and the rest of the family, add an "I love you," and you're done. Then pop it into an envelope, get a stamp, and mail it. Yes, it takes a little longer than e-mail, but the joy you'll give—and receive—will last ten times as long.

What Are You Proud of Today?

Whether you realize it or not, you did at least one thing today that you should feel good about. Maybe you did a whole lot more, but let's just start with one. At the end of every day, write down something you did that you're proud of—doing good work on a test, helping a friend, finishing a book, playing hard for your team, holding a door open for someone, trying a new food. Keep a list—include anything and everything you feel good about. Every item is proof that you are growing and maturing into the person you want to be. Congratulate yourself and challenge yourself to see how long your list can get. You won't believe how many great things you've done, and can continue to do.

You *Can* Be on Time

Why is it that some people are always late, and others always manage to be on time? Have you ever noticed how late people always have an excuse—the bus didn't come, the bathroom was too crowded, there was a long line at the drinking fountain—instead of admitting they're just late? Few things are as annoying to others as someone who's always late, keeping others waiting. And who knows what you're missing?

Lateness is a bad habit, just as punctuality is a good

Tiger Woods with Fred Couples, 1992.

habit. Create a good habit for yourself and build it into your life. Being on time shows responsibility, and it's not hard to accomplish if you make a simple plan. Make a list of everything in your schedule that requires you to be somewhere on time—the school bus, your classes, after-school activities, dinnertime. Then make a commitment to get where you need to be, on time. At the end of the day, check off those that you got right and take a good look at those you missed. You can get it right the next day. Try not to be late for the same thing twice. You will gain the respect of others—and yourself—very quickly.

Open Up

It's scary to share our feelings with others. After all, who wants to admit when we're sad, or angry, or jealous, or scared? It seems easier to keep those feelings safely locked inside, secret and private, so no one will think we're weak or immature. But what if sharing those feelings could actually make things better? Your friends might feel exactly as you do, but if nobody talks about it, nobody wins. So take the first step. By showing that you're confident enough to open up and admit your feelings, you give others the power to do the same. Now you can begin to share ideas about how other people handle their lives, and you can learn and grow from their experiences, just as they can benefit from yours. You are not alone in this world. Share yourself with others.

TIGER SAYS . . .

"My father has always taught me that there are only two things in life that you have to do. You have to share and you have to care."

Friends Don't Own Each Other

Do you get upset when your best friend has plans with someone else? Is your friend hurt when you do something that doesn't involve him or her? What a great way to ruin a friendship. Friends who grab on and refuse to let go aren't showing that they care; they're showing that they're insecure and don't have faith in the friendship. A true friend is confident enough to know that each of you can have other friends and interests, and still be best friends at the end of the day. Try this: The next time your friend wants to include other people, or makes plans that don't involve you, give him or her the freedom to do so. If your relationship is solid, it won't matter, because true friendships survive anything.

The Big Cleanup—What Can You Donate to a Good Cause?

The fact that you're growing as a person also means you're outgrowing things as well—books you've already read, clothes that are too small, shoes that don't fit, toys and games you never play with anymore. Why not put them to good use by sharing them with those less fortunate? Make a positive contribution to someone else's life by donating your useful items to someone who really needs and appreciates them. Yes, it's hard to give up things that have been special to you, but think about kids who don't have *anything* special. Wouldn't it be great if someone else could appreciate and enjoy the things you can't really use anymore? There are countless charities that are just waiting to find good homes for wonderful, gently used items. Share and care.

Write a Letter to a Government Leader about a Concern You Have

There are people who complain about the problems in our world, but make no attempt to change anything. And then there are the people who realize that they have the power to make a difference. Which are you?

Each of us has the power, kids included, and it starts with a single voice—yours! Maybe there's a problem in your neighborhood that affects you, like a run-down park, or a street that's too dangerous for you to cross, or drugs in your school. Maybe there's a bigger national problem that has your attention, like homeless children or gun control. You may not be old enough to vote, but you are old enough to speak out about issues that concern you. Fortunately, we live in a democracy with certain freedoms guaranteed. One of these is the freedom of speech. Not only is it your right to contact a government representative about something that is important to you, it's your *responsibility*. Are you willing to sit back and hope that someone else is speaking out? Can you afford to? Your opinion matters—share it with those who can do something about it. What are you waiting for?

Lose Like a Winner

Life is filled with competition, big and small. Playing in the big game, trying out for a show, running for school office, qualifying for the honor roll . . . someone will go home happy, and someone won't. Competition exists everywhere, and what's wrong with that? After all, we can only be the best that we can be. Acknowledge that, and move on. There's pride in winning, but there's pride in losing, too, if you tried your best.

True winners know how to lose gracefully. When Tiger was eleven, he was playing in the Junior World Championships, expecting a victory because he had won two first places and a second in three years. This time, however, he didn't finish in the top five, which would have qualified him for a trophy. Was he disappointed? Absolutely. But when the trophies were presented to the top five winners, he walked up and congratulated each one—without any suggestion from me. I knew then that he could handle defeat as well as success; he knew how to lose. He acknowledged that he had done his best, but on that day, someone else was better. You can win by losing, if you learn from your loss and treat the winners with respect.

TIGER SAYS . . .
"How can you finish second and feel relieved? I enter every tournament with the same thought: win. If I don't, I'm disappointed, but it doesn't

take long to get over it, and I learn from the experience."

Who Are Your Real Friends?

I'm sure you know people who are nice, fun to be with, and share your interests. They might be in your class or hang out with your other friends. You enjoy being with them. Are these true friends? Maybe someday, but for now, they're more like acquaintances. A true friend is so much more, and extremely rare; if you're lucky, you'll have three or four real friends in your entire life. That doesn't sound like a lot, but if you understand the real meaning of friendship, you'll realize how lucky you'll be to have those few.

What makes real friends stand out? They are there for you, right or wrong, good and bad. They give you the truth when others can't or won't. You can count on them for anything, anytime, throughout a lifetime of trust and respect. Can you say that about everyone you hang out with today? Probably not, but you have to start somewhere.

Choose your friends very carefully. Real friends don't drag you down, judge you, push you around, or make you feel bad. They support your decisions and your values and stand by you when you need support. Anyone who can't do these things for you isn't worthy of being your friend.

Control Your Anger

Go ahead, get mad. Anger is an emotion, and like all emotions, it bursts out whether you want it to or not. The question is, how do you handle this powerful emotion? Do you go crazy, throwing things and screaming your head off? Or do you stop, think, and try to work it out? If you're a thrower/screamer, maybe you need to think about controlling your anger, before you do some damage you can't undo.

There are three steps to controlling your anger: (1) Admit that you're angry. Just shout it out: "I'm so mad!" (2) Realize that it's all right to be angry. After all, something caused your anger, so don't make yourself wrong. (3) Now you have a choice. You can continue to be angry until you get over it, whenever that might be, or you can choose to be something else: calm, annoyed, understanding, sad, accepting, forgiving, whatever. The choice is yours. If you choose to stay angry, that's all right, too, because now you have the power to replace the anger with something else any time you want. Now you can control your anger instead of your anger controlling you. You must follow the steps in the exact order, though, or it won't work. If you do, you'll find a world of difference in your life.

The Family Collection Box

Here's a way for the whole family to work together to make a difference. Create a special box or jar for loose change, contributions from your allowance, whatever anyone wants to give. At the end of each month (or week, or year—it's up to you), hold a family meeting and decide how to put the money to good use in the community. You can buy holiday gifts for needy children, hats or gloves for the homeless, books for a school or library, stuffed animals for sick kids in the hospital. Use your imagination, and give from the heart.

Keep Your Promises

It's so disappointing when someone lets you down, isn't it? You have plans with a friend, but he decides to do something else. Someone promises to loan you something, but never follows through. It really damages your trust in that person. So if you don't like it when others break their promises to you, make it a point to never do it to them. Let your word be your honor and be faithful to what you say—*come from truth!*

Of course, sometimes we have no choice but to change our plans, and that might mean disappointing someone. Be honest and open—no excuses, just the truth—and let the other person know when and how you'll make good on that promise. You can be counted on. You can be trusted. Wouldn't you want all your friends to be faithful to you? Before you expect it of them, you have to do it yourself.

Should You Cover Up for a Friend Who Breaks the Rules?

What a terrible situation: your friend cheated on a test, or took something from a store without paying, or did something else that you know was wrong. And to make things worse, this "friend" is mad at you because you didn't do it, too! Do you go along with your friend so he or she won't be mad at you? Do you look the other way and pretend you don't know or care? Do you tell your friend to knock it off? Or do you report the crime?

First of all, anyone who would ask you to compromise your own integrity and sense of responsibility is *not* a true friend. If you allow others to suck you down to lowering your standards and values, then you become like them and give up your power as an individual. Second, you have a responsibility to let your friend know that (*a*) you won't go along with it, and (b) you won't cover it up. The definition of friendship does not include an obligation to make it easy for your friends to do something wrong. If you want to be a real friend, be honest and caring, and help your friend find the way back to the truth. If you believe that reporting the situation is the right thing to do, then do it. But never let yourself be dragged down by someone else's bad choices. You are each responsible for your own actions.

Showing Off Is Not the Same as Showing Confidence

Nobody likes a show-off. You know the type: They're always bragging about something they did, how great they are, how much better they are than everyone else. But those people aren't showing confidence; they're showing the exact opposite. They're telling the world they're so insecure that they need to constantly convince others of their successes. Confident people are proud of their accomplishments without announcing them to everyone and anyone who'll listen. They feel good about themselves, and they feel good about others as well. Confidence gives you the ability to walk into a room and feel strong and comfortable, sure of who you are, without feeling the need to broadcast that you're better than everyone else. You are a beautiful person and people will see that for themselves.

TIGER SAYS . . .

"My dad has always had a big belief in my abilities, and so have I. The only difference is he stated them and I didn't. I let my clubs do the talking."

Share Your Talents

You are a unique individual, with your own special talents and abilities. Some of us are good golfers or spellers; some of us can skateboard or draw cartoons. But something that comes easily to you might not be so easy for someone else. So when you realize your talents, also realize that you can (and should) share them with others. Show your friends a trick that works for you, a technique that might help them improve their skill. Maybe your friends can teach you a few things as well. We're all teachers, and we're all students. You have special gifts. Share them.

TIGER SAYS . . .

"One of my goals and passions is to help people and I love doing it. I've always tried to help and give back to golf as much as I can. It means

*a lot to me that kids can get a chance and suc-
ceed if they want to."*

Just Do It—Volunteer

This is your chance to show the world the wonderful
person who exists in you. By volunteering—standing
up and saying, "I'll do it!"—you show that you care
about people and the world around you. And there
are so many easy ways to show it. At home: volun-
teer to play with your little brother, put groceries
away, put photos in an album. At school: offer to
help the teacher after school, organize a cleanup project, raise your hand when you think you know the
answer. With your friends: show a new kid around
the neighborhood, help your friend with his math
homework, teach him that cool yo-yo trick. Don't
wait for the world to come to you. Reach out for

new exciting things to do—you won't believe how good you'll feel about yourself. Sure, it's easier to sit in the corner and not be noticed, but what does that say about you? Join the group and show what you're capable of. We're waiting for you.

TIGER SAYS . . .

"My dad has always taught me to care about others, and I try to share my success in any way I can."

Say You're Sorry

The following is *not* an apology: "Okay already, I'm sorry, I said it, are you happy now?" If that sounds like you, well, you could use a little work on your apology skills.

Why is it so hard for some people to say they're sorry? Instead of just admitting they're wrong, they have a pack of excuses and a list of people to blame. "It's not my fault. . ." "How was I supposed to know. . ." "That's not what happened. . ." For some reason, these folks can't just say, "I'm sorry," as if an apology might take something away from them or make them look weak. But the opposite is true: strong, confident people have no problem saying "I'm sorry." It shows you're big enough to admit when you're wrong, and that you have the compassion and sensitivity to care about the feelings of others.

A true apology comes from the heart, real and genuine. It never comes with an excuse—nothing ruins an apology like a long, lame explanation. Just say you're sorry, and mean it.

Forgive Someone

Somewhere, at this very minute, there is someone out there who hurt you, angered you, upset you . . .

and you still haven't gotten over it. Someone talked about you behind your back, your friend canceled plans with you to hang out with someone else, a kid in class made fun of you, your brother took something of yours without asking. Well, you're entitled to feel hurt or angry, and those feelings can last a long time, because as tough as it can be to say "I'm sorry," it can be just as tough to say, "I forgive you." But if the person who hurt you can apologize—not an easy thing to do—you can make an effort to forgive, especially if the apology is sincere, real, and from the heart. Forgiveness is not a sign of weakness; it shows your power as an individual. It doesn't mean you're "giving in," or giving the other person permission to hurt you again. It means that you're strong enough to accept the fact that everyone makes mistakes, and your friend is no exception. It takes nothing away from you as a person—it adds to your strength.

"I'm so bored . . ."

Next time you're sitting around with nothing to do, make a list of twenty-five things you can do the *next* time you have nothing to do. Your list can range from productive (clean out your desk drawer, make cookies, start a new book), to silly (learn to juggle, have a bubble-blowing contest, see how many words you can make out of the letters in your name). Just making the list will fill some time. Then the next time you need an idea to fill a lazy day, check the list. You might even accomplish something.

Ask Other People about Themselves

Isn't it boring when someone always talks about himself and never shows any interest in anyone else? Not only does it make for a dull, one-sided conversation, it's just plain rude. Take the time to show interest in others—it's a great way to get people interested in you. Why? Because it shows that you care about others, that you have an active, curious mind, that you're not self-centered and always thinking me-me-me. Not only will you open the gateway to new relationships, you might learn a few things as well. Asking people about themselves doesn't make you look nosy, it makes you seem confident enough to show interest in others. "What are you doing this summer?" "How do you hit that ball so straight?" "How's your new dog?" "Where did you get that cool haircut?" "Can you show me how to draw that?" So many ways to start a conversation, launch a friendship, and show you care. Don't be afraid to try it.

Interview Your Grandparents and Parents about Their History (It's *Your* History, Too)

Long before you appeared on this planet, there were other kids just like you, having fun like you, with troubles just like you. These kids had hopes and dreams and disappointments and successes, and lots of important decisions to make, just like you. You even know some of them—they're your grandparents, parents, aunts, and uncles, and the stories they can share will blow you away. Maybe they fought in wars or came to this country with nothing in their pockets. Maybe they had some of the same hopes and dreams you have and overcame amazing obstacles. How did your grandparents meet? What was their school like? What did they do for fun? What do they recall about being a kid? Ask them! Not only will you learn some incredible things, but the person you're interviewing will be truly grateful for your interest. Try getting your conversation on videotape, or a tape recording, to create a wonderful, permanent record of these special people. Your family history is such a big part of who you are—get to know it.

Say What's on Your Mind

Are you a mind reader, able to guess what everyone is thinking all the time? No? Then why do you expect others to know what's on your mind? If you're disappointed or mad at someone, it only makes it worse to bottle it up inside, give the silent treatment, ignore the person, and expect him or her to "get the message." Get what message? What message can they possibly get, except that you're not honest about your feelings, and unable to communicate about what's bugging you?

Use the power of truth. Face your problems and

differences and clear them up so you can get rid of the bad feelings and get back to life.

Parents Are People, Too

You're not perfect and neither are your parents. Believe it or not, they have fears and concerns and pressures that might even be bigger than yours: problems at work, paying the bills, and even dealing with *their* parents. Instead of expecting them to concentrate only on you, take a minute to concentrate on them. Ask your mom about something that's important to her; ask your dad if he had a good day. And don't forget to tell them you love them—often. They will appreciate it more than you'll ever know.

Who Are You Trying to Please?

If you find yourself making decisions so that others will like you and approve of you, instead of doing what feels right for you, you need to ask yourself why. Are you hoping to be noticed by the popular kids? Afraid your friends will drop you if you're not just like them? Worried about hurting your parents if you don't listen to their advice? Well, what about listening to your heart? Don't you owe it to yourself to think about what *you* really want?

Yes, it's important to consider the opinions of people who care about you; after all, your friends and family might have a view you haven't considered. But if you've really thought it through, and you have good reasons for feeling the way you do, then trust yourself. Your real friends will respect you for standing up for what you believe in, and your parents will love you no matter what. Remember: If something doesn't feel right, it probably isn't.

Earn Your Parents' Respect and Trust

There is only one way to gain respect and trust, and that is to earn them. Nobody is going to give them to you without a solid daily effort. If you want your parents to trust you, you have to show that you can be trusted. Do your chores and your homework. If you're supposed to be home by ten, be there. If you make a promise, keep it. Tell the truth. Show respect—you'll get respect back, and you'll have earned it.

Your parents don't sit around looking for ways to spoil your fun. But they do have the right—and the responsibility—to be on the lookout for situations that might not be good for you. They may trust you completely, but still have some doubts about the rest of the world—the kids you're hanging out with, the safety of the place you're going, the reliability of your ride home. You may disagree, and probably will, but you owe it to them to consider why they might feel the way they do. Then it's up to you to either accept their judgment, or work with them to show why they should trust yours. Either way, it's a two-way street. Believe this: They really do want to trust you. Give them the chance, and watch your relationship grow closer and more solid every day.

TIGER SAYS . . .

"When I was younger, my dad and I would sit and talk for hours. That's how we built up trust and respect for each other."

When It's Time to End a Friendship

People change, and so do relationships. Maybe your old friend is hanging out with new kids you don't feel comfortable with. Maybe your friend hasn't been treating you right, or hasn't been there for you lately. Maybe you just don't have fun together anymore. Just because you've been friends since first grade doesn't mean you have to stick with it forever, especially if the friendship isn't working for you. It's okay to move on. You don't have to break off the relationship forever—you probably have a lot of great memories together—but you can keep your distance and spend time with other people. Established relationships never really end, they just change shape. Be honest with yourself, trust your instincts, and you'll know what to do.

Your Time Is Valuable—Protect It

How many times has this happened to you: you sit down to study, or read a book, or just watch TV . . . and you get interrupted by someone or something that needs your attention *right now!* Your best friend calls to chat, the kids down the street want you to come outside to play ball, your little brother wants to tell you some jokes. Before you know it, the valuable time you set aside to do something is gone.

What should you do? Well, how about putting yourself first once in a while? It's okay to say no, and it's not that hard to do. Commit a specific amount of time to your own plans before you start, and stick to your commitment. Then tell your friends you'll be free in twenty minutes, or an hour, or however much time you promised yourself. After all, if you don't take yourself seriously, who will?

Give Yourself a Break

Like everyone else, you have a breaking point, when your talent, patience, concentration, strength, and desire just run out. You can't read one more word, hit one more ball, practice another minute. In short, you need to take a break. It takes honesty and confidence to admit that you've hit the wall and, even more important, to take a timeout for yourself *before* you hit the wall. When Tiger became a professional golfer, he learned quickly that he couldn't compete every week, *and* give clinics, *and* make public appearances, *and* take care of business commitments, *and* work on his game, *and* still have a life. He realized that he needed time to recover from the stress of competition, prepare for upcoming tournaments, and just hang out. And if that meant missing opportunities to compete, or turning down offers that cut into his time, it was worth the sacrifice. Make the same sacrifice for yourself. Work hard, play hard, but take time to recharge your batteries. After all, you're only human, so why try to be anything else?

TIGER SAYS . . .

"I know my limitations and try to schedule days off in between playing golf and other commitments so I don't get burned out."

Earn Money Doing What You Love

You may not be old enough to go out and get a real job, but there are plenty of ways to make some money doing things you already enjoy. If you love little kids, visit your neighbors who have children and offer your services to baby-sit, take kids to the park, organize a small playgroup. If you love to play sports, organize a little clinic for younger kids, and help them with their skills. If art is your passion, set up a small studio at home where other kids can learn from you. If you like to work outside, you can mow lawns or weed gardens. But don't wait for the business to come to you—get out there and earn it. Print up flyers to put in neighborhood mailboxes, describing your service, how much you charge, and why you'll do a great job. Whatever you charge, be fair and reasonable, and remember to put part of your earnings aside for your favorite charity.

TIGER SAYS . . .

"I get to play golf for a living. What more can you ask—getting paid for doing what you love."

When a "Friend" Is No Friend

No way around it, some people just don't know the meaning of friendship. One minute you're having fun together, and the next minute they're talking behind your back, telling everybody what's wrong with you, stepping all over your feelings, and generally making you feel lousy. Unfortunately, they don't have the maturity or common sense to know how to relate with others, and you can't change them—not unless they want to change. But you *can* change your reaction to them. Instead of trying to "win" back a friend with a bad attitude, make up your mind to put some distance between you and find other people to be with. Yes, it hurts, and will probably make your ex-friend act even worse, but consider this: Why waste your time on someone who can't appreciate the value of respect and kindness? Wouldn't you rather be with people who make you happy and share your idea of what makes a solid friendship? You deserve friends who care about you and support you, not tear you down. Knowing the difference can change your life.

Support Your Teammates
(Especially When They Really
Need It)

Remember the last time you struck out or dropped a pass or missed a free throw? You didn't do it on purpose, but you still wanted to disappear. It can be so embarrassing to mess up in front of your teammates, especially if you have teammates who think it's their job to point out your mistakes, yell at you, and generally make you feel worse than you already do. Remember that awful feeling the next time someone else has a bad day, and do something positive for your hurting teammate. Everyone goofs up or has a bad day, and you don't need to remind him; humiliating people doesn't make them play better. Instead, reach out and let them know that you're on their side. A few nice words ("Don't worry about it, you'll get 'em next time" . . . "You can do it" . . . "Good try!") can make a world of difference to someone who really needs some support. Show yourself and others that you value people over winning. Wouldn't you want someone to do that for you?

Surprise Someone

A funny note in your friend's backpack, an unexpected phone call to Grandpa, an extra job around the house to give your parents a break—what a way to make someone's day. Make it part of your day, too, by showing the people you care about that you're thinking of them. You might even inspire them to do the same for someone else—or for you when you really need it.

Make the First Move

You and your friend had a fight, and now you're not speaking to each other. And since each of you is positive that the other is wrong, you're both sitting back and waiting for an apology. Now ask yourself this: Are you prepared to lose the friendship over this disagreement? If yes, congratulations, because that's what's going to happen. If not, be the bigger person, and break the ice. You don't have to accept all the blame or responsibility, but you can agree to disagree: "I'm sorry that we can't agree on this, but I respect your opinion and care about your friendship more than I care about this fight. Can we put it behind us?" It takes confidence and courage, but the reward—a better friendship—is worth it.

Change a Bad Habit

Biting your nails, telling fibs, eating too much candy, using bad language . . . some people might consider these bad habits. Do you? Because unless you're ready and willing to change something about yourself, there's no chance it can happen. You are the only person who can decide to kick a habit. Even Tiger, who occasionally develops bad golf habits that affect his game, can't change the habit until *he* decides it's necessary, no matter what the "experts" tell him.

Change comes because *you* want it to. So if you're ready to make a change, here's a plan: Create new habits. Old habits don't just disappear, they are just replaced by new habits. When you're about to do the same old thing, replace it with the new action. For example, when you're about to tell a lie, stop and count to ten, using the time to think of something else to say. Instead of swearing, make up a new word to substitute for the word you're trying to lose. When you feel like biting your nails, pop a piece of gum in your mouth or shove your hands into your pockets until the urge passes. Then commit yourself to repeating the new habit over and over again until the old habit gradually fades away and becomes nonexistent. It's hard work, but you can do it if you really want to.

TIGER SAYS . . .
"I truly believe if you concentrate hard enough, good things happen."

Share the Holidays with Those in Need

What better way to celebrate the holidays than to give to those who aren't as fortunate? Instead of waiting for the gifts to roll in and the celebration to start, think about others who have much less than you. Talk to your family about what you can do to brighten the holiday season for those in need. There are so many ways to reach out and help: spend an afternoon volunteering at a homeless shelter, bring cookies to a nursing home, make goody bags filled with activities for hospitalized kids who can't be home for the holidays. Or instead of spending all your holiday money on each other (do you *need* all those gifts?), discuss how you can spend it on others: Buy toys for kids who won't get any, canned goods or grocery gift certificates for the hungry, or monetary donations to any charity you believe in.

You can do the same thing on your birthday by asking for a gift to be donated in your name to a favorite charity so another kid can enjoy the things you like. Or ask your friends to bring a can of food (or other necessities) to your birthday party, so that you can donate them.

Giving from the heart will make your own holidays so much more meaningful, and doing it with your family will start a tradition you'll always remember.

If You Don't Want All the Blame, Don't Take All the Credit

Any time you're involved in a team effort—a class project, a sport, any kind of group activity—remember that you're all in it together. What if your team lost or did poorly on the project: Would you be willing to take all the blame? No? Then don't take all the credit. It doesn't matter if your contribution was spectacular; if everyone contributed in some way (even a small way), then everyone deserves to share the glory. No one wants to hear you saying, "If it weren't for me, we would have lost" or "I did the most work on this." Have the confidence to know in your heart that you did a great job, and be proud of yourself for it. And let everyone feel proud too. A true leader makes an effort to be sure that everyone feels appreciated and important—it makes the whole team stronger.

Make a Plan

If you were going to drive from California to New York, you'd look at a map, wouldn't you? That's just how you set goals for yourself. You create a map or plan that will help you achieve whatever you desire in your life. Major goals or minor goals, the key is to decide how to get from point A to point B. Tiger has consistently established goals for himself throughout his entire life—very high goals that he shares with no one but himself. A big part of his success is that his expectations for himself are so much higher than anyone else could ever have for him, so he doesn't spend much time worrying about what other people expect. He just focuses on his own dreams, and never takes his eyes off the target.

You can do the same. Select one of your goals, big or small, and list the steps you need to take to get there. What's the first step? Then what? Make a plan and follow it, step by step, always keeping your goal in sight. You'll be amazed by how much closer it will seem, if you can see exactly how to get there. Just remember, these are *your* goals, and no one else's. Dream big!

TIGER SAYS . . .

"One of the things my parents taught me is never listen to other people's expectations. You should live your own life and live up to your own expectations. Those are the only things I care about."

What Are You Afraid of?

Okay, let's just all shout it out: *We all get scared.* Yes, every one of us, even the coolest kid in school, even your parents, even Tiger Woods. Everyone is afraid of something—we're just built that way. The question is, do your fears keep you from growing and accomplishing things? Are you afraid to try out for the team or a show because you're not sure you'll make it? Afraid to go to a party because you might not know anyone there? Afraid to start a conversation with someone you'd like to know better because they might not be interested?

Ask yourself, "What's the worst thing that can happen?" The usual answer is that the world won't crash to an end, and neither will you. If you don't make the team or get the part, you'll be disappointed, but you can learn from the experience and improve your chances for next time. And won't you always wonder what might have happened if you had tried? So you might not know anyone at the party, but you might meet some new people, and in the worst case, you can always leave. As for striking up that conversation with someone you think might reject you, just remember that it's their loss, not yours, if they're not interested. Having the confidence to admit your fears makes those fears easier to tackle. You don't fail when you fall down, you fail when you don't get back up.

TIGER SAYS . . .

"Ever since I was a little kid, I always believed in my ability to compete on the golf course. I don't know why. I've just always believed in what I can do. Win or lose, I've always given it everything I have."

Don't Believe Everything You Hear

If you stacked up everything written and reported about Tiger (or any other celebrity) , and then compared it all to the real story, you would never believe you were hearing about the same person. Tiger is surrounded by so much misinformation, rumor, guesswork, and gossip that if he had to take the time to deny and explain it all, he'd have no time left for anything else.

So what does this have to do with you? Every day, you're surrounded by information that you're supposed to believe: news reports on TV and radio, newspapers, magazines, the Internet. Wherever you go, you hear stories from your friends and family that you probably believe. But should you? Stop and think. Ask questions: "How do you know that's true?" If something doesn't sound quite right, maybe it isn't.

Intelligent people like you can find things out for themselves—they don't believe everything they're told. It's your responsibility to decide for yourself what you're willing to believe, and what might just be a rumor or misrepresentation of the real story. There are two sides to every story (and sometimes more), so don't make up your mind about someone or something until you've asked questions and learned all there is to know. And if you can't get enough information, you can choose to not believe what you heard. Be fair, be curious, and above all, never stop looking for the truth.

TIGER SAYS . . .

"Interesting. . . . People always seem to know more about my life than I do."

Be "Someone"

"Someone should do something!" How many times have you heard that? Someone should clean up that park! Someone should report those wild kids! Someone should help that homeless family! Someone, someone, someone. Well, aren't you someone? Instead of expecting "someone" else to get things done, get busy, get involved. If you're not able to do it alone, get some friends or an adult to help you. If the park needs to be cleaned up, form a group and do it. If a bunch of bullies are acting like jerks, report them. If you know of people in need, help them. If you can stand up and take some action, others will follow. You can make a difference in the world you live in, one action at a time. What a great way to really be "someone."

The Kid Who Won't Be Your Friend

Face it: You don't like everyone, and everyone doesn't have to like you. No doubt about it, it hurts when someone is rude to you or ignores you, but think of it this way: It's their loss, not yours. Their bad attitude is no reflection on you. Sometimes, no matter how hard you try, you're just not going to connect. So now what? You have a few choices: You can continue to try to make friends with this person, in which case you'll probably spend a lot more time feeling bad. Or you can understand that for now, he or she is obviously not right for you and missed a great opportunity to have you for a friend. Stay proud and confident; stand firm on who you are, with full knowledge that you're a good person. Never, ever allow anyone to take that away from you. And finally, make sure you never act that way toward anyone else. Everyone deserves the courtesy of kindness.

TIGER SAYS . . .
"If you truly love yourself, then everything will be okay."

Talent Minus Hard Work
Equals Zero Success

No one owes you anything. No matter how talented you are, if you're waiting for the phone to ring with offers for you to be class president, team captain, the star of the show, or a straight-A student, you're going to wait a long time. Any success you'll ever have will come because of talent and hard work, and even if you have the talent, you still won't get anywhere without the hard work. Being smart doesn't guarantee good grades if you don't study. A great athlete can't win anything if he isn't prepared to compete. Your great acting ability will never be recognized if you don't practice and prepare. Talent only guarantees that you're good at what you do; hard work gives you a shot at greatness.

TIGER SAYS . . .
"To be honest with you, there's just no substitute for hard work. There are no shortcuts."

Respect the Opinions of Others, Even When They're Completely, Insanely, 100 Percent Wrong

What an amazing country we live in: Everyone gets to have an opinion, and every opinion is protected by law, no matter how unpopular. But there's a catch: If you want others to respect your ideas, you have to respect theirs. Sorry, but that's the way it works. You may believe with all your heart that your opinion is absolutely, positively, the only right answer, but you don't get to decide for anyone else. We're all different, so why should everyone have to think like you? Dare to disagree. We all get to be right, if only in our own minds. Have the confidence, maturity, and inner strength to know that your beliefs are solid, and you don't need everyone else to agree in order to feel right. That's the very essence of democracy, and it's the foundation of this country. Without it, nothing works.

Read the Newspaper

Even if you watch the news on TV, even if you check out news stories on the Internet, make time every day to read a newspaper. Newspapers are absolutely bursting with ideas and information that you can use in so many ways, and that can get you thinking about things that never crossed your mind. And they're already customized for you, with sections on all different interests. Did you know that all the words in a half-hour TV broadcast would fit in two columns of a newspaper page? Every newspaper is loaded with details and stories that TV and radio can't begin to cover over their limited airwaves, and those details are what make it possible for you to understand and appreciate what's really going on around you. If you only get your news online, you're probably just clicking on the headlines that you're already interested in, without realizing everything else that's there. But when you look at a newspaper, you can't help but discover things you didn't know existed. You don't have to read every page or every section, but read something, every day. It's your right and privilege. Exercise it.

Say Thank You

It costs nothing and means everything. Saying thanks is so simple, so basic, so necessary. And if you don't think it really matters, conduct your own experiment: For an entire day, pay attention to whether people thank you for the nice things you do. Whether you hold a door for someone, or give a friend a piece of gum, or help a classmate with a math problem, watch and see if you get thanked. By the end of the day, you'll get the message: When you do something nice, it feels good to be acknowledged, and even makes you want to do more. And what about the people who didn't bother to say thanks? Don't they seem rude and self-centered? Take the time—one tiny second—to appreciate the people who show you kindness and courtesy. They deserve it . . . and so do you.

Do Your Part to Stop Racism and Prejudice

Any intelligent person knows that it's wrong and ignorant to dislike people because of their religion, skin color, or culture. How can anyone feel entitled to look down on others when we're all from the same race, the human race? Yet as long as there are people who feel they're superior to others, racism and prejudice will continue to exist. The question is, what can *you* do about it?

Start by opening your mind and heart to people who are different from you. Get to know them, learn from them, and let them learn from you. Refuse to tolerate racist attitudes in others: You don't have to listen to closed-minded people who spread their negativity around like a bad smell. Challenge them to appreciate and accept others for who they are—what a boring world this would be if everyone was the same. Don't put up with racist or ethnic jokes, even when the "joker" makes fun of himself or uses that weak excuse, "It's just a joke." Jokes that make fun of someone's heritage or culture are just pitiful excuses for insulting people.

We all belong here, and we all have to learn to live together. The time to start is now. Be the person who starts it. You can't change the whole world by yourself, but you can start with yourself and move on to your home, your friends, your community. Believe in your ability to set a good example for others, and just watch how many lives you can affect.

Celebrate Yourself

You have powers that you haven't even discovered yet, deep inside you, waiting for you to release them. Let them out. Use them to make a difference in your life and in the lives of others. You have the power to care about others, to make solid, responsible choices, to stand up for what you believe. You have the power to dream amazing dreams, and turn them into reality. You have the power to set goals that only you can achieve. You are a miracle, and you can make miracles happen. Celebrate yourself, love yourself, for all the things that make you special and unique. Remember: You are the greatest, and there's only one of you. Become a role model. *Start something!*

TIGER WOODS FOUNDATION, INC.
Our Mission

The Tiger Woods Foundation envisions a world where people of varying backgrounds, histories, races, languages, and ethnicity can reach their highest potential and participate fully in the economic and social mainstream of society.

We shall adopt as our own the very traits embodied in Tiger Woods: courage, creativity, work ethic, tenacity, integrity, heart, self-esteem, and drive for excellence.

The Foundation will actively encourage and promote parental responsibility and involvement in the lives of children and celebrate the spirit of inclusion in all aspects of human existence.

The Foundation will work to achieve its objectives in a number of ways. These include recognizing the family as the basic, most important unit in society, and identifying the role of the parent as the most important teacher in the life of any child. We shall conduct golf clinics in major metropolitan areas in the United States for young people historically denied access and exposure to the sport, support programs that promote educational achievement and job opportunities for inner-city and other disadvantaged youth, and participate in programs and events that promote racial harmony and help people understand and appreciate the value of inclusiveness.

The Tiger Woods Foundation is a 501 (C) 3 nonprofit organization (Federal ID No. 06-1468499). If you'd like to make a donation to help support our activities, please send a check payable to:

Tiger Woods Foundation, Inc.

P.O. Box 550

Reynoldsburg, OH 43068-0550